SIMPLE TRADITIONAL
ORIGAMI

TOMOKO FUSE

JAPAN PUBLICATIONS TRADING COMPANY

Published by Japan Publications Trading Co., Ltd.,
1-2-1 Sarugaku-cho, Chiyoda-ku, Tokyo, 101-0064 Japan

First edition, First printing: September 1998

Distributors:

United States: Kodansha America, Inc. through Oxford University Press,
  198 Madison Avenue, New York, NY 10016.
Canada: Fitzhenry & Whiteside Ltd.,
  195 Allstate Parkway, Markham, Ontario L3R 4T8.
United Kingdom and Europe: Premier Book Marketing Ltd.,
  1 Gower Street, London WC1E 6HA, England.
Australia and New Zealand: Bookwise International,
  54 Crittenden Road, Findon, South Australia 5023, Australia.
The Far East and Japan: Japan Publications Trading Co., Ltd.,
  1-2-1 Sarugaku-cho, Chiyoda-ku, Tokyo, 101-0064 Japan.

10 9 8 7 6 5 4 3 2 1

ISBN 4-88996-041-4

Printed in Japan

CONTENTS

List of Color Illustrations

1

2

3

4

5

19

20

21

22

23

30

31

32

33

34

35

36

37

38

39

41

40

42

43

44

45

Symbols

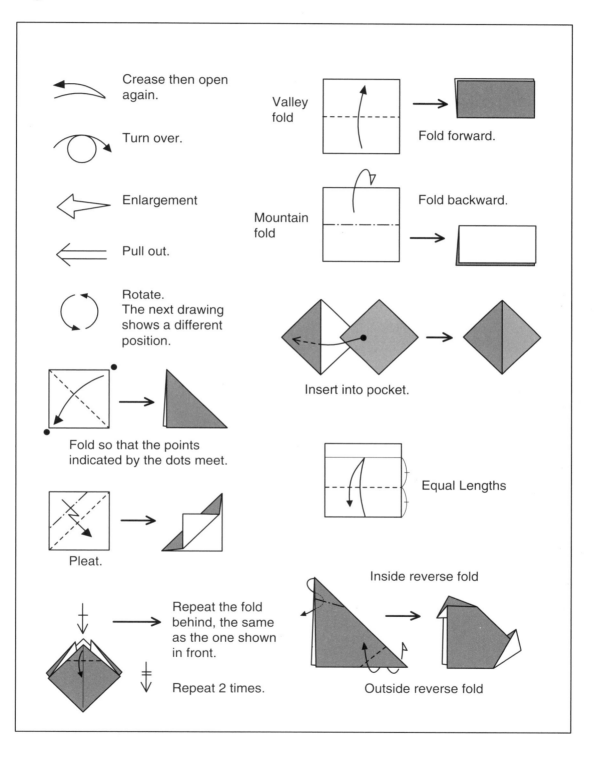

Crease then open again.

Turn over.

Enlargement

Pull out.

Rotate.
The next drawing shows a different position.

Fold so that the points indicated by the dots meet.

Pleat.

Repeat the fold behind, the same as the one shown in front.

Repeat 2 times.

Valley fold

Fold forward.

Mountain fold

Fold backward.

Insert into pocket.

Equal Lengths

Inside reverse fold

Outside reverse fold

Cup

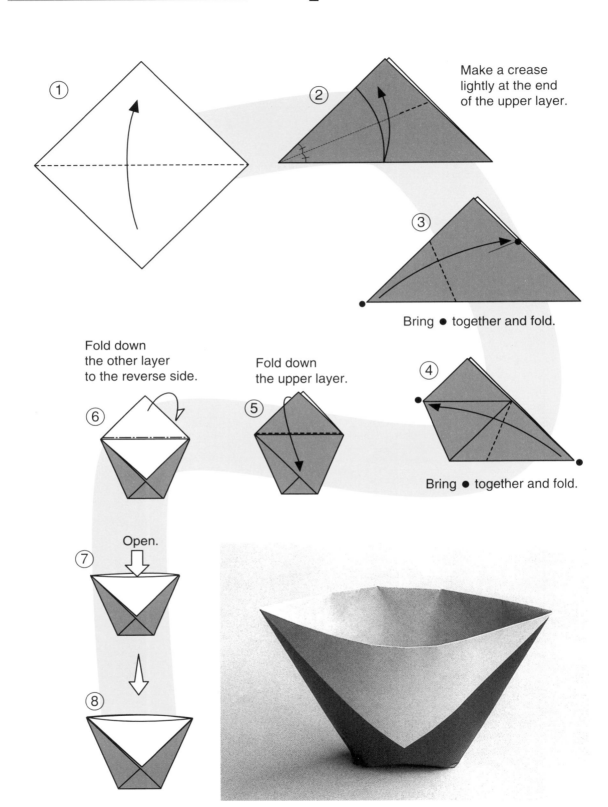

①

② Make a crease lightly at the end of the upper layer.

③ Bring ● together and fold.

④ Bring ● together and fold.

⑤ Fold down the upper layer.

⑥ Fold down the other layer to the reverse side.

⑦ Open.

⑧

14

Butterfly

Simple folding. The butterfly flies down turning round and round.

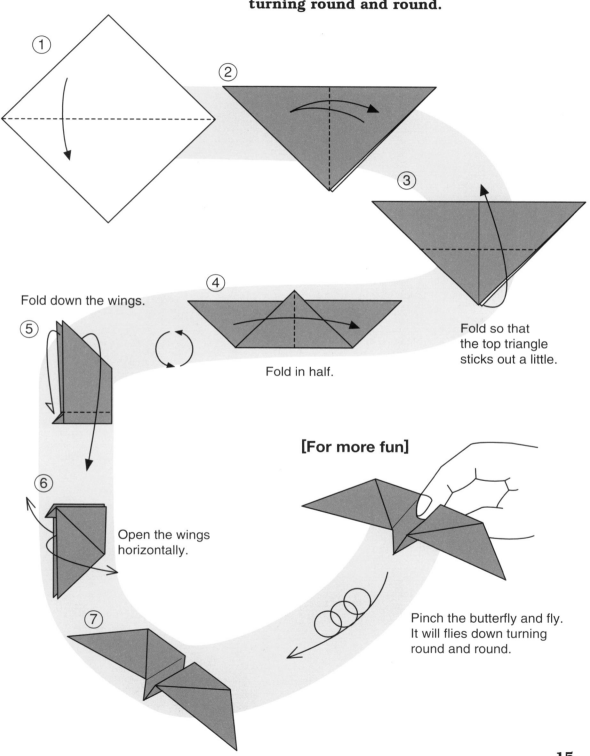

①

②

③ Fold so that the top triangle sticks out a little.

④ Fold in half.

Fold down the wings.

⑤

⑥ Open the wings horizontally.

⑦

[For more fun]

Pinch the butterfly and fly. It will flies down turning round and round.

Cicada

①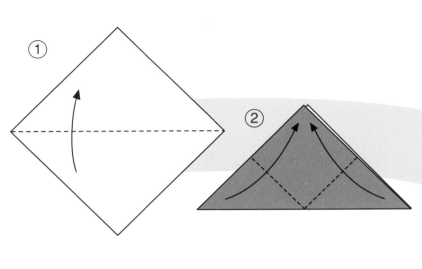

Fold down the wings, shifting the tips of the triangles a little bright and left.

②

③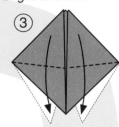

④

1/4

Fold down the upper layer at 1/4.

⑤

Fold down upon the upper layer, shifting a little.

⑥ Fold behind.

⑦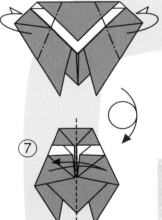

The crease in the center makes it look like a cicada.

⑧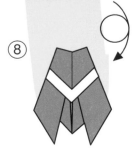

House & Piano

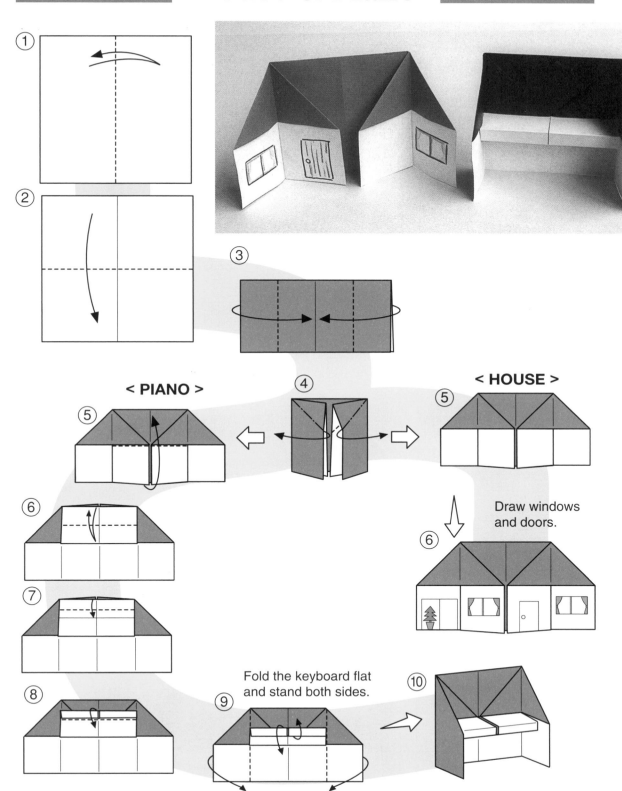

①

②

③

④

< PIANO >
⑤

⑥

⑦

⑧

Fold the keyboard flat
and stand both sides.

⑨

⑩

< HOUSE >
⑤

Draw windows
and doors.

⑥

Stand for Placing Offerings

A container with handles.

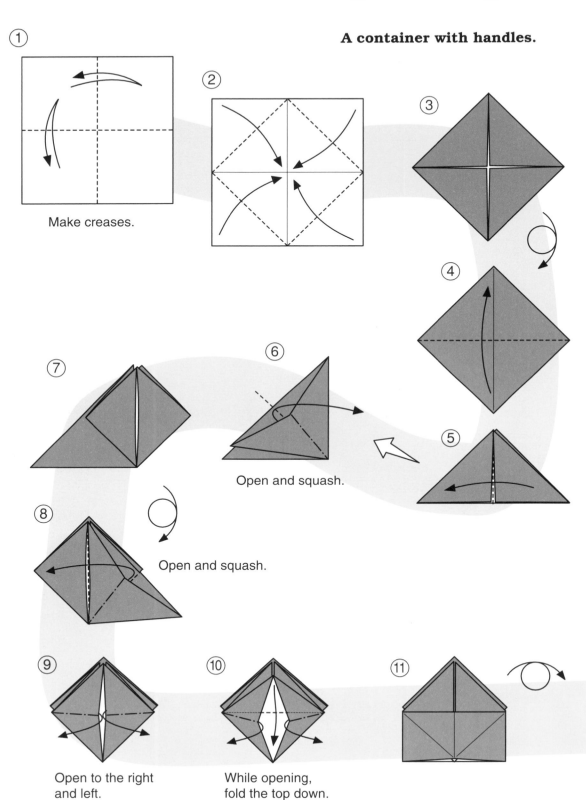

① Make creases.

②

③

④

⑤

⑥ Open and squash.

⑦

⑧ Open and squash.

⑨ Open to the right and left.

⑩ While opening, fold the top down.

⑪

18

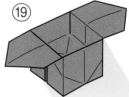
⑲

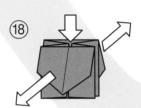
⑱

Draw handles and
open the inside.

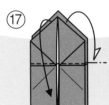
⑰

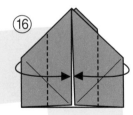
⑯

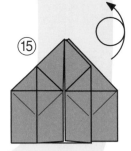
⑮

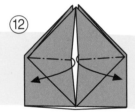
⑫

Do the same on the reverse
side as in steps ⑨ and ⑩.

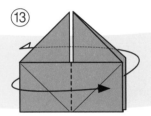
⑬

Rotate flaps.

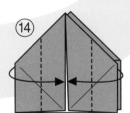
⑭

Container & Mouth

This container turns out a mouth, which opens
and closes with fingers.
It will be interesting to draw a face or patterns.

①

②

③

④

⑤

⑥

⑦

Open and squash.

⑧

⑨

Open and squash.

⑩

Pull out the four tips.

< CONTAINER >

⑪

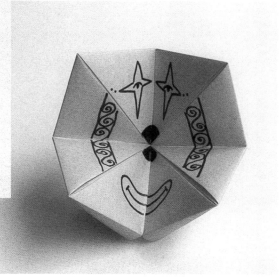

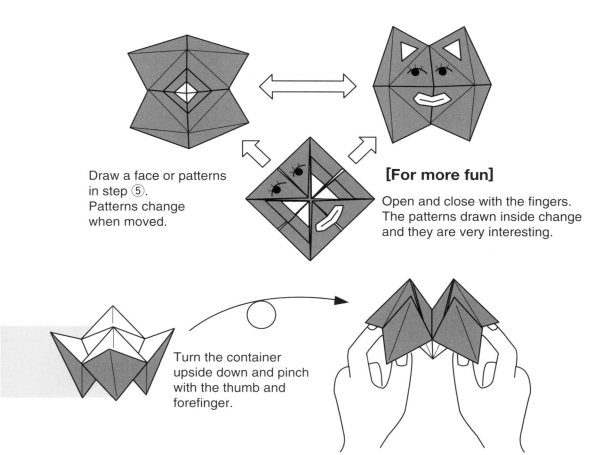

Draw a face or patterns in step ⑤.
Patterns change when moved.

[For more fun]

Open and close with the fingers. The patterns drawn inside change and they are very interesting.

Turn the container upside down and pinch with the thumb and forefinger.

Hungry Crow & Story Teller

(by Tomoko Fuse)

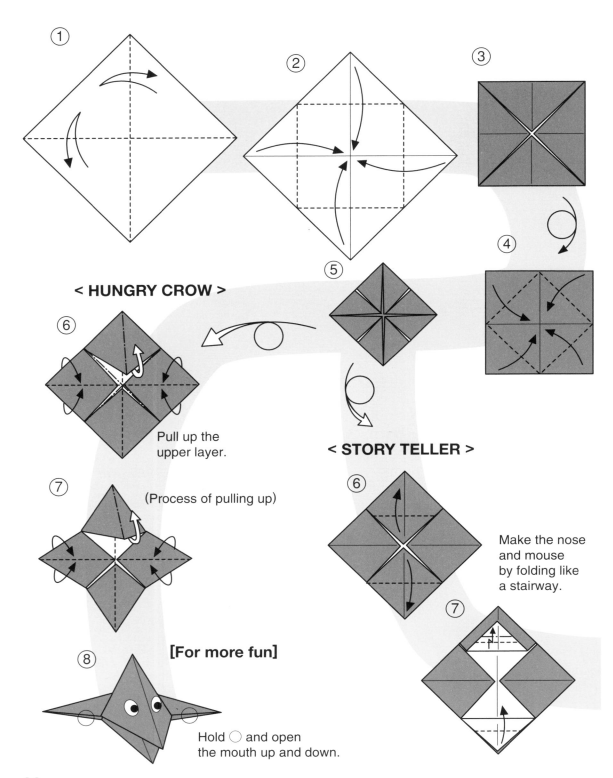

< HUNGRY CROW >

⑥ Pull up the upper layer.

⑦ (Process of pulling up)

⑧ [For more fun]

Hold ◯ and open the mouth up and down.

< STORY TELLER >

⑥ Make the nose and mouse by folding like a stairway.

⑦

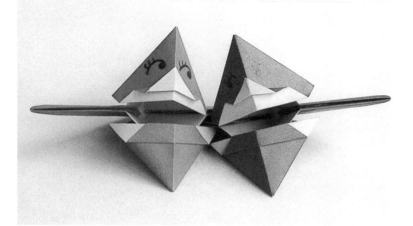

Hold ◯ and open
the mouth up and down.

⑪

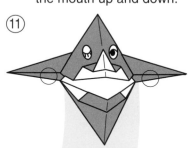

Draw a face
and beard.

Pull out the top and
bottom layers.

⑧

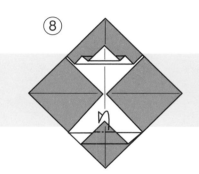

⑨

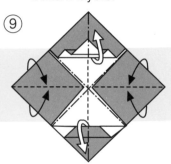

⑩

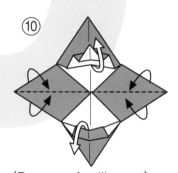

(Process of pulling out)

Pretty Bird

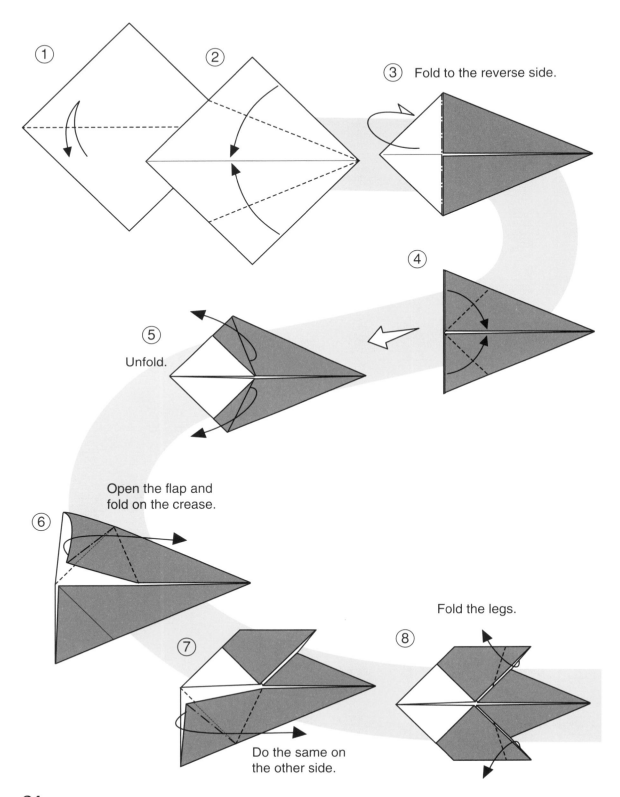

①

②

③ Fold to the reverse side.

④

⑤ Unfold.

Open the flap and
fold on the crease.

⑥

⑦ Do the same on
the other side.

Fold the legs.

⑧

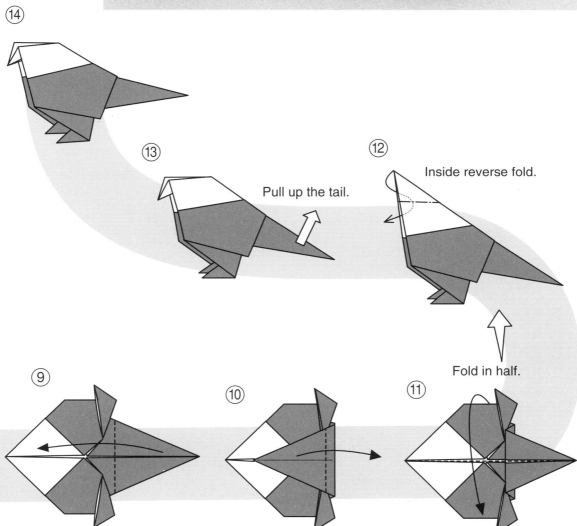

⑭

⑬

Pull up the tail.

⑫

Inside reverse fold.

⑨

⑩

⑪

Fold in half.

25

Jumping Frog

This frog really jumps.

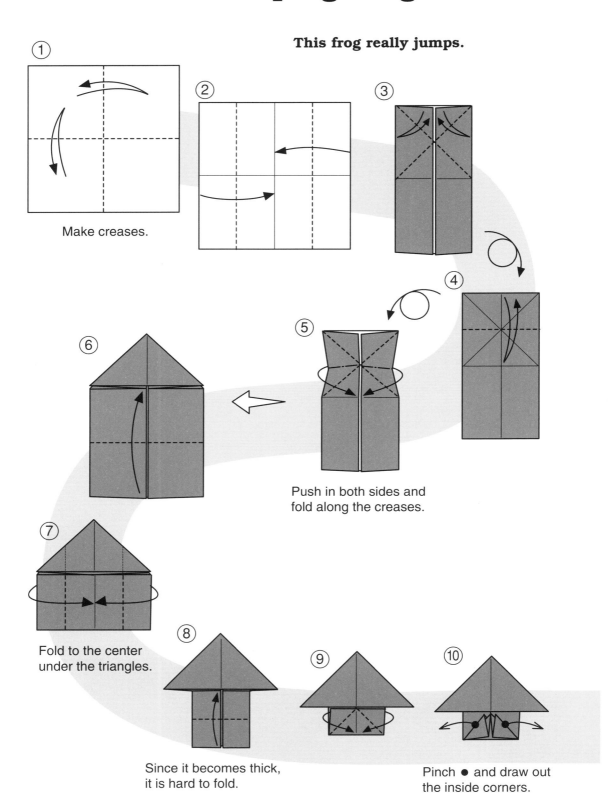

① Make creases.

②

③

④

⑤ Push in both sides and fold along the creases.

⑥

⑦ Fold to the center under the triangles.

⑧ Since it becomes thick, it is hard to fold.

⑨

⑩ Pinch ● and draw out the inside corners.

[For more fun]

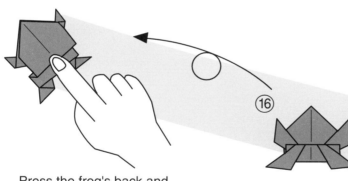

Press the frog's back and
legs together.
Slide the finger off
and the frog jumps.

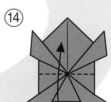

Since it becomes
too thick, it is
hard to fold.

(Process of drawing out)

Fur Seal

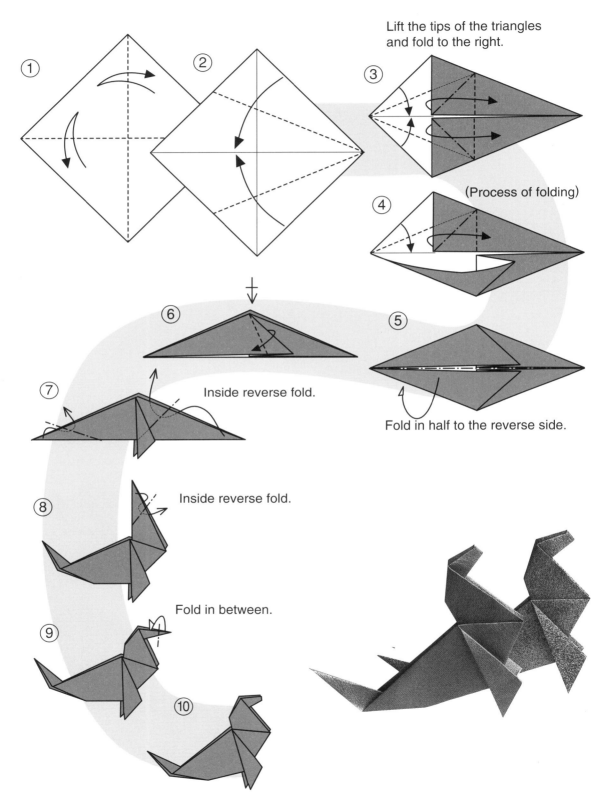

Lift the tips of the triangles and fold to the right.

① ② ③

(Process of folding)

④

⑥ ⑤

Inside reverse fold.

Fold in half to the reverse side.

⑦

⑧ Inside reverse fold.

Fold in between.

⑨

⑩

Pigeon

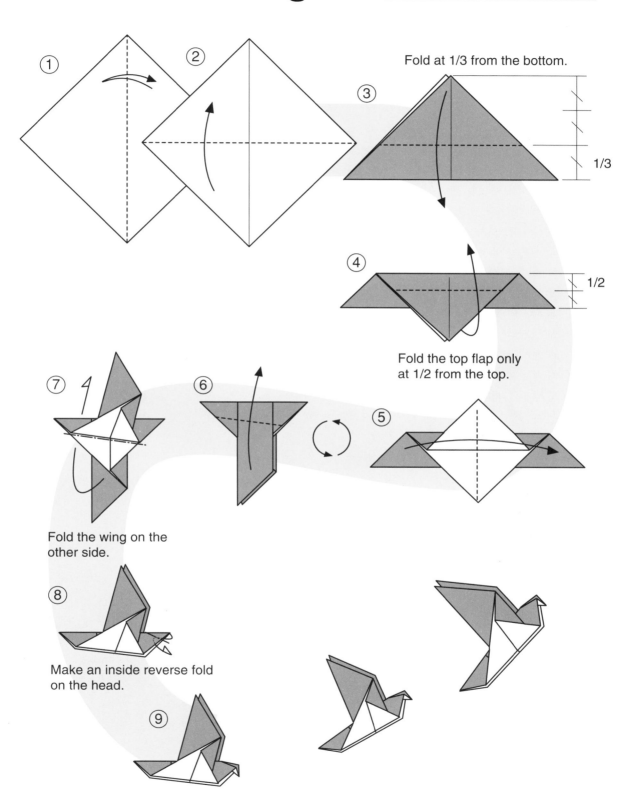

①

②

③ Fold at 1/3 from the bottom.

1/3

④ 1/2

Fold the top flap only
at 1/2 from the top.

⑤

⑥

⑦

Fold the wing on the
other side.

⑧

Make an inside reverse fold
on the head.

⑨

Casket with Horns

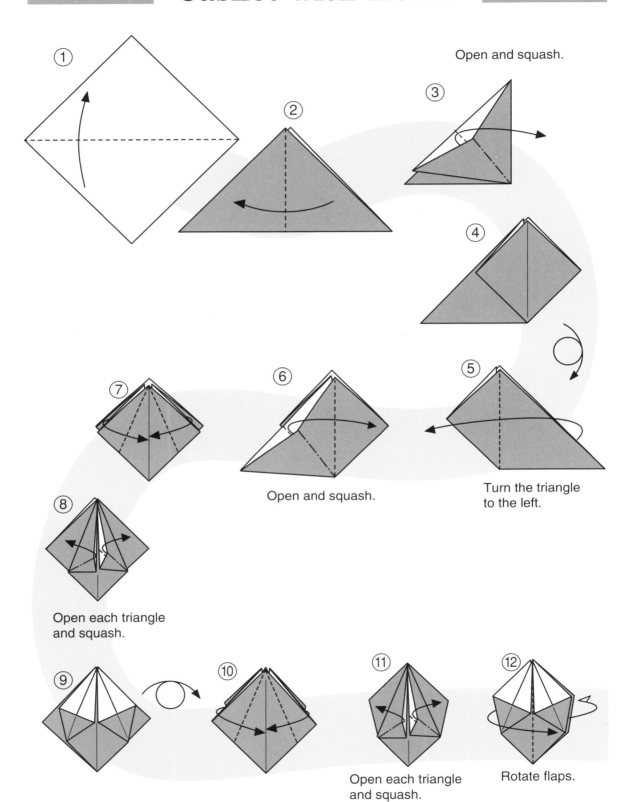

①

②

③ Open and squash.

④

⑤ Turn the triangle to the left.

⑥ Open and squash.

⑦

⑧ Open each triangle and squash.

⑨

⑩

⑪ Open each triangle and squash.

⑫ Rotate flaps.

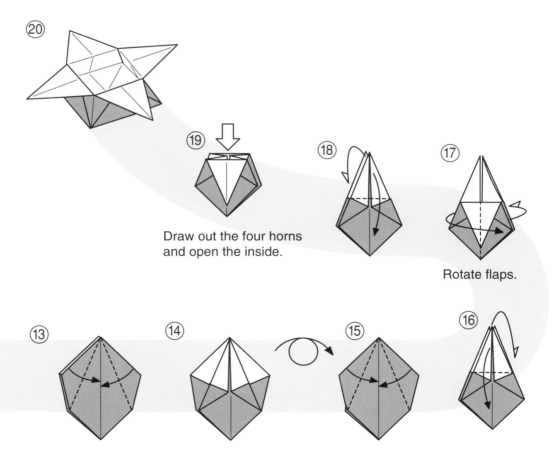

⑳

⑲

Draw out the four horns
and open the inside.

⑱

⑰

Rotate flaps.

⑬

⑭

⑮

⑯

Church

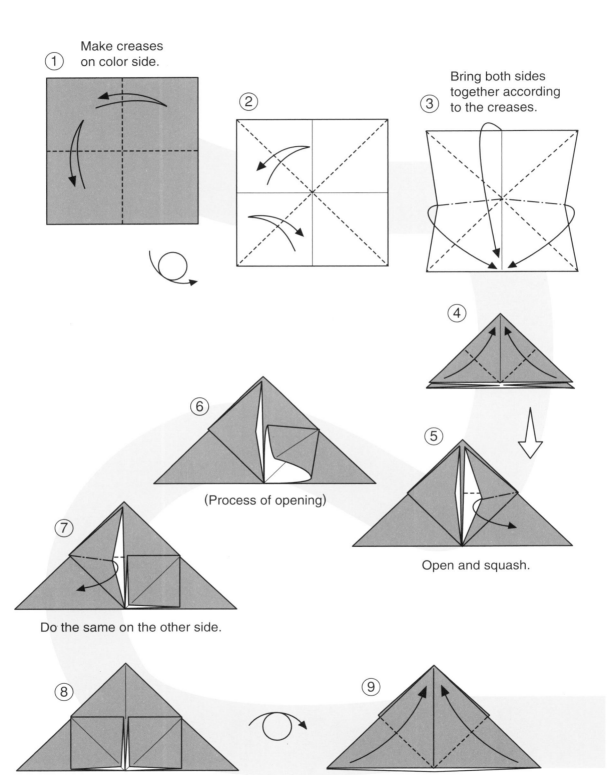

① Make creases on color side.

②

③ Bring both sides together according to the creases.

④

⑤ Open and squash.

⑥ (Process of opening)

⑦ Do the same on the other side.

⑧

⑨

32

⑯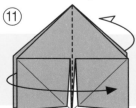

↓ Fold the reverse side
in the same way.

⑮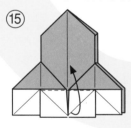

↓ Fold the reverse side
in the same way.

⑭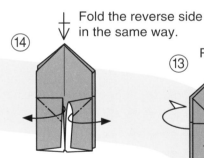

Rotate flaps.

⑬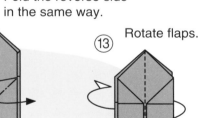

Open and squash.

⑩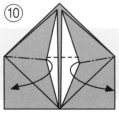

Rotate flaps.

⑪

Fold the reverse side
in the same way.

⑫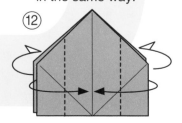

Bird that drinks water

A delightful bird that drinks water.
A Chinese traditional origami.

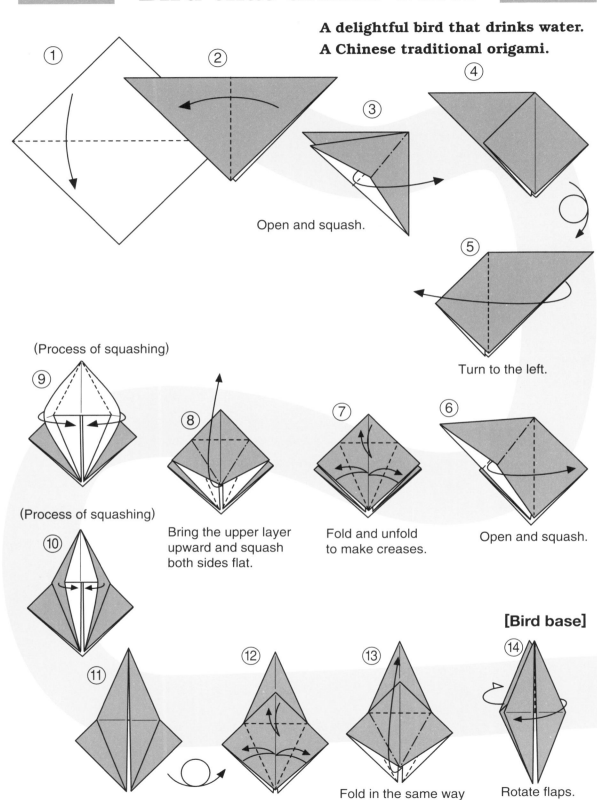

①

②

③ Open and squash.

④

⑤ Turn to the left.

⑥ Open and squash.

⑦ Fold and unfold to make creases.

⑧ Bring the upper layer upward and squash both sides flat.

⑨ (Process of squashing)

⑩ (Process of squashing)

⑪

⑫

⑬ Fold in the same way as step in ⑧ .

⑭ Rotate flaps.

[Bird base]

34

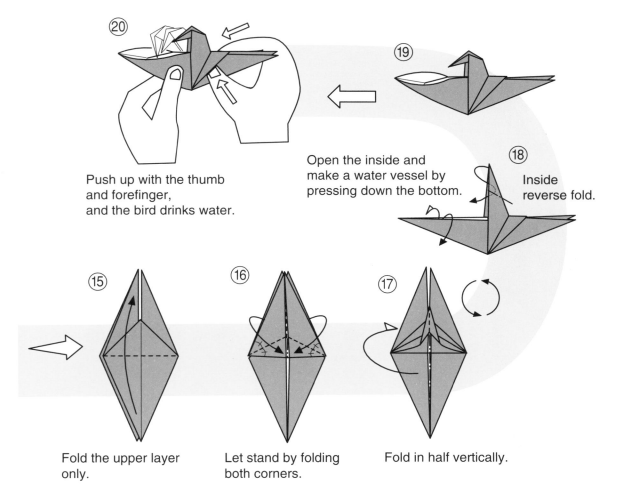

⑳

Push up with the thumb
and forefinger,
and the bird drinks water.

Open the inside and
make a water vessel by
pressing down the bottom.

⑲

⑱ Inside
reverse fold.

⑮

Fold the upper layer
only.

⑯

Let stand by folding
both corners.

⑰

Fold in half vertically.

Crane

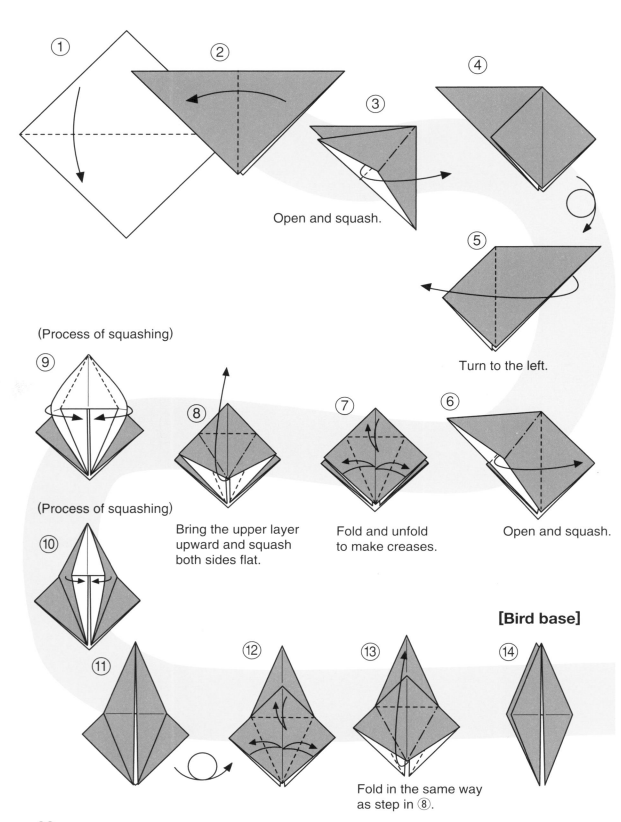

(1)

(2)

(3)
Open and squash.

(4)

(5)
Turn to the left.

(6)
Open and squash.

(7)
Fold and unfold
to make creases.

(8)
Bring the upper layer
upward and squash
both sides flat.

(9)
(Process of squashing)

(10)
(Process of squashing)

(11)

(12)

(13)
Fold in the same way
as step in (8).

(14)

[Bird base]

36

Flapping Bird

From the [Bird base] on page 36.

Pull and release the tail. The wings flap. This bird is the symbol of BOS (British Origami Society).

Inside reverse fold.

①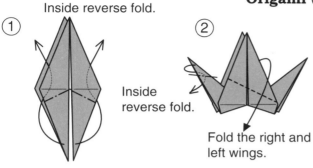

Inside reverse fold.

② Fold the right and left wings.

③  Hold ● and pull and release the tail. The wings flap.

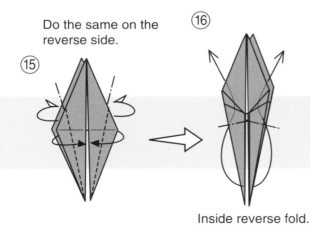

⑲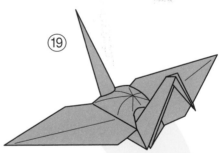

⑱  Pull wings apart and inflate the body.

⑰ Inside reverse fold to make the head.

⑯ Do the same on the reverse side.

⑮

Inside reverse fold.

Puppy

by Tomoko Fuse

A cute puppy.

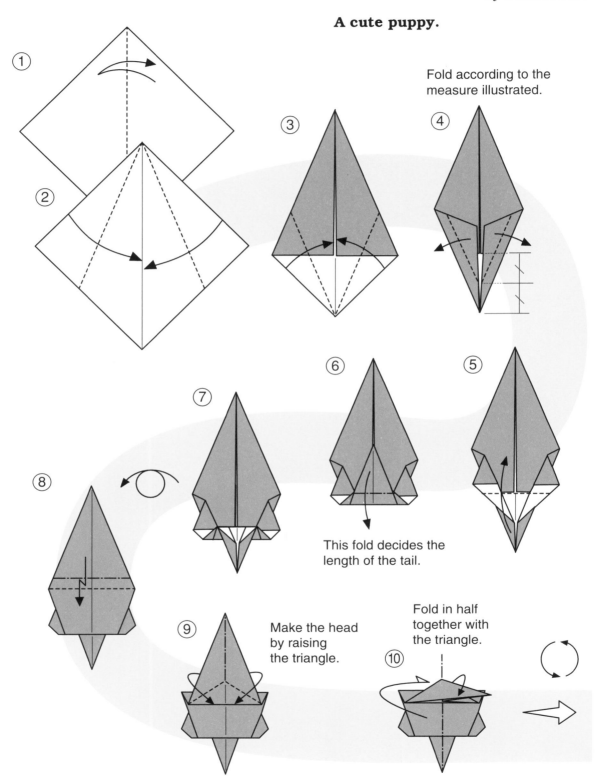

Fold according to the measure illustrated.

This fold decides the length of the tail.

Make the head by raising the triangle.

Fold in half together with the triangle.

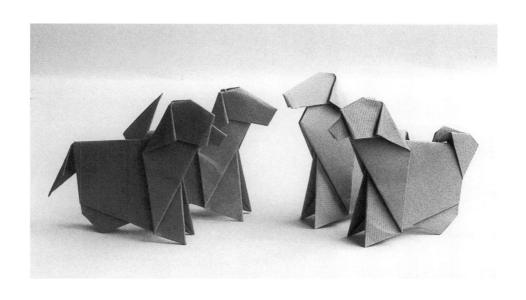

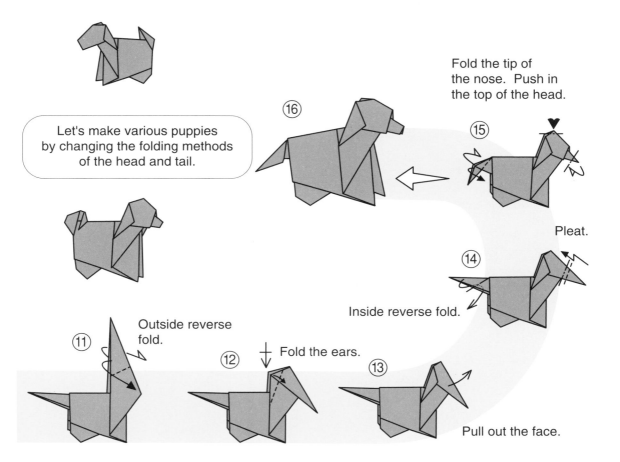

Fold the tip of
the nose. Push in
the top of the head.

⑯

Let's make various puppies
by changing the folding methods
of the head and tail.

⑮

Pleat.

⑭

Inside reverse fold.

Outside reverse
fold.

⑪

⑫ Fold the ears.

⑬

Pull out the face.

Tiny Turtle

by Tomoko Fuse

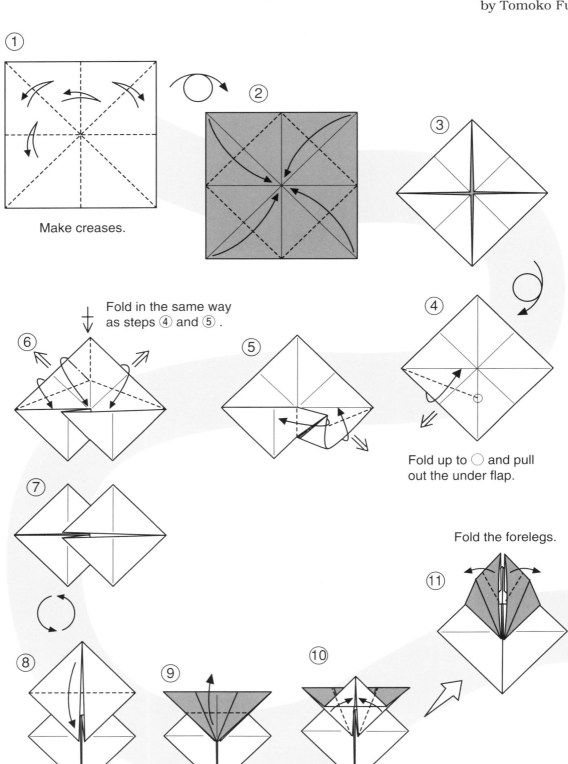

① Make creases.

②

③

④ Fold up to ○ and pull out the under flap.

⑤

⑥ Fold in the same way as steps ④ and ⑤ .

⑦

⑧

⑨

⑩

⑪ Fold the forelegs.

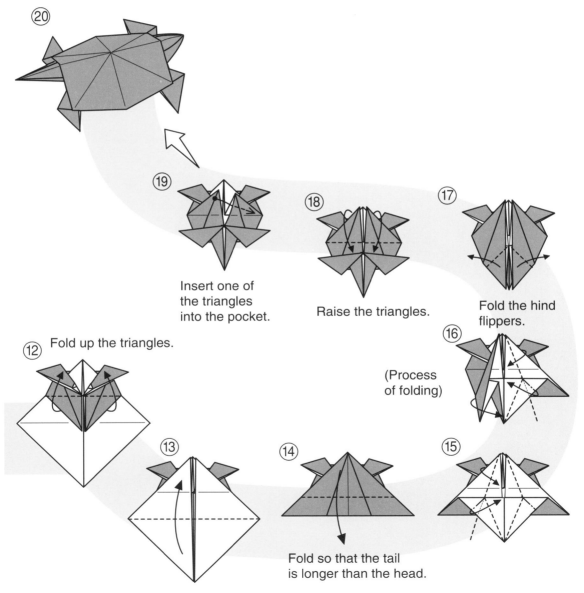

⑳

⑲ Insert one of
the triangles
into the pocket.

⑱ Raise the triangles.

⑰ Fold the hind
flippers.

⑯ (Process
of folding)

⑫ Fold up the triangles.

⑬

⑭ Fold so that the tail
is longer than the head.

⑮

Viking Ship

It is exciting to give the last finish at one stroke. You will never be tired of folding this ship.

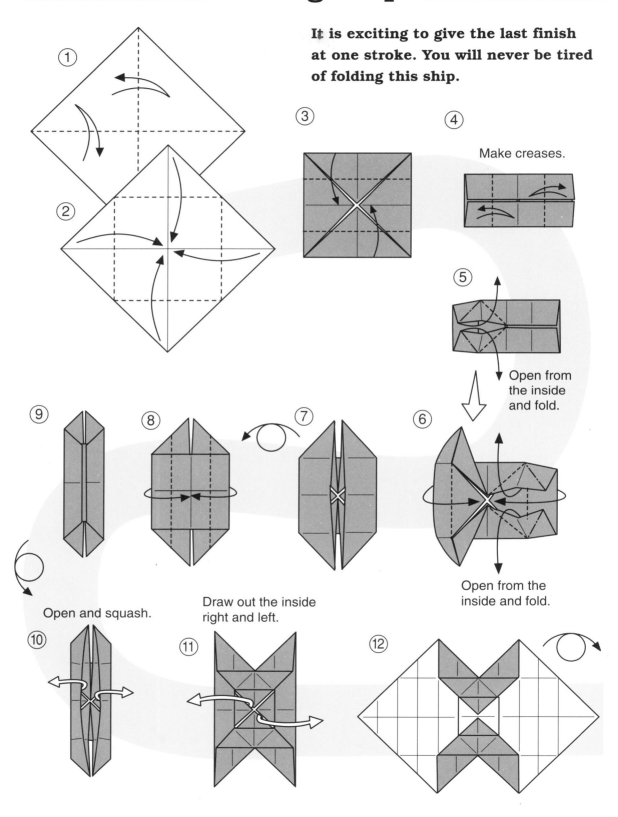

Make creases.

Open from the inside and fold.

Open from the inside and fold.

Open and squash.

Draw out the inside right and left.

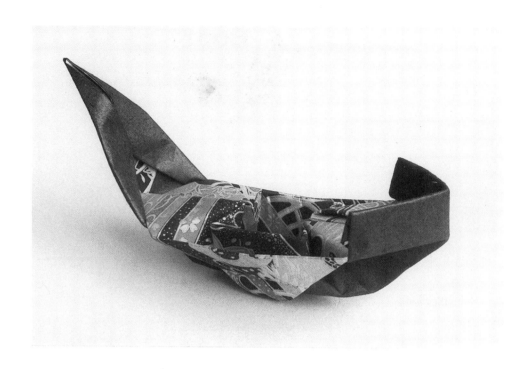

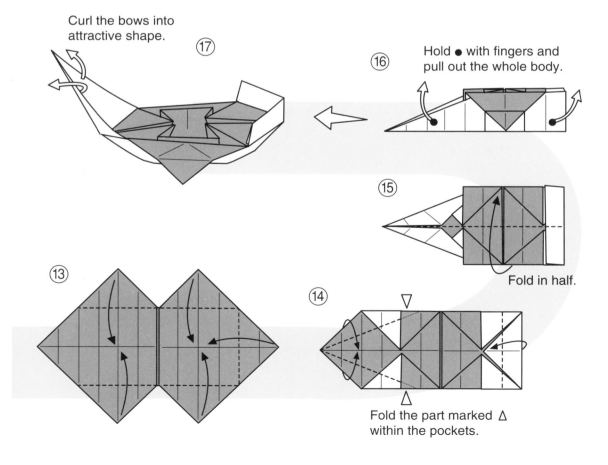

Curl the bows into attractive shape.

⑰

Hold ● with fingers and pull out the whole body.

⑯

⑮

Fold in half.

⑬

⑭

Fold the part marked △ within the pockets.

Boat

**Step ⑦ is difficult,
but you will be pleased with the result.**

①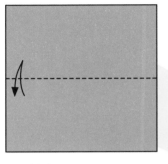

Make a crease
on color side.

②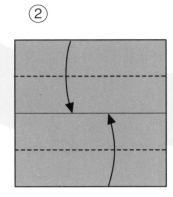

③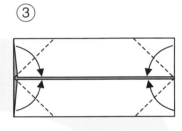

④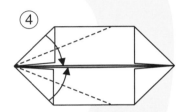

⑤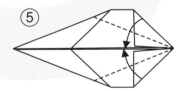

⑥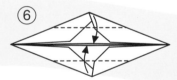

⑦

Turn the inside out.

⑧

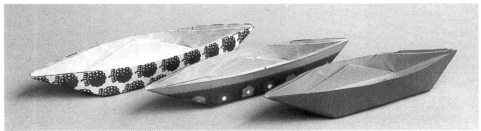

44

Motorboat

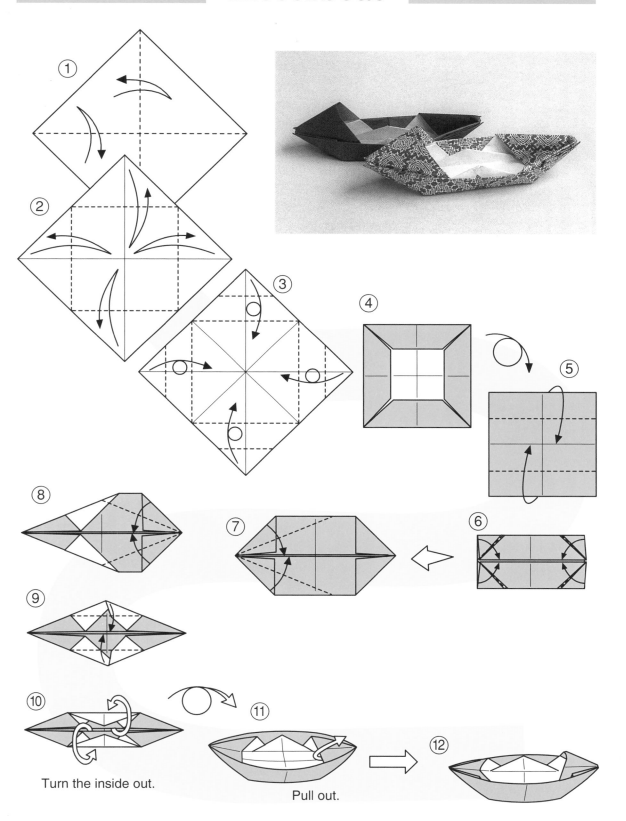

①

②

③

④

⑤

⑥

⑦

⑧

⑨

⑩ Turn the inside out.

⑪ Pull out.

⑫

Mountain-climbing Monkey

Chinese traditional origami. If you rub the paper, the monkey of a triangle climbs the mountain and flies out.

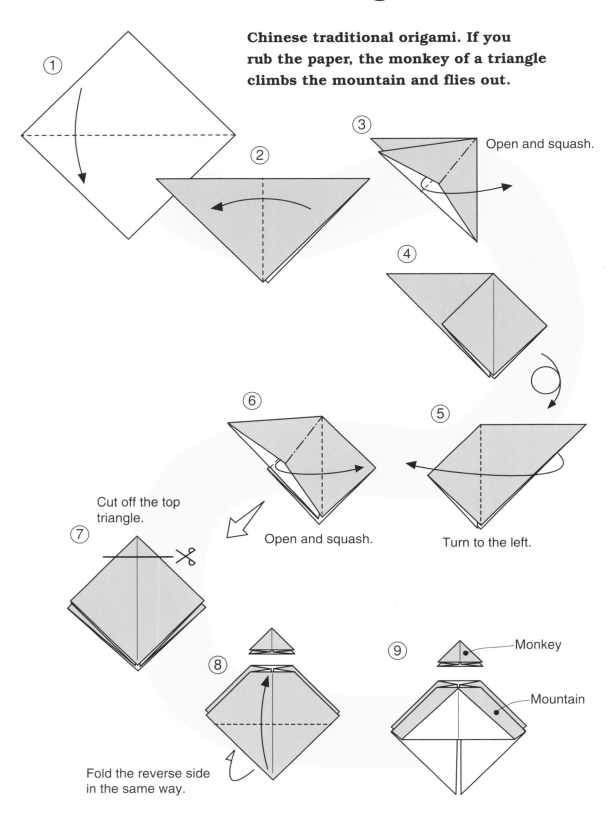

①

②

③ Open and squash.

④

⑤ Turn to the left.

⑥ Open and squash.

⑦ Cut off the top triangle.

⑧ Fold the reverse side in the same way.

⑨ Monkey

Mountain

46

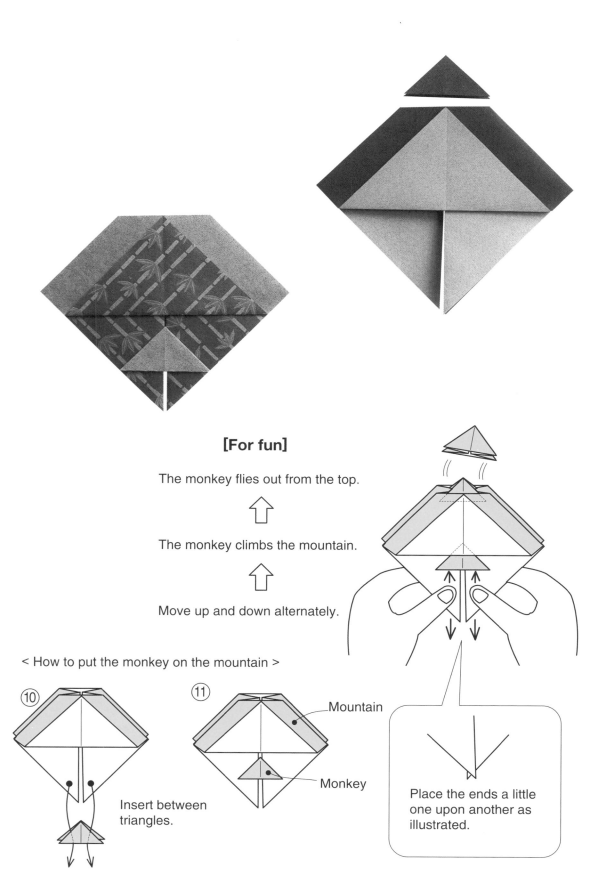

[For fun]

The monkey flies out from the top.

⇧

The monkey climbs the mountain.

⇧

Move up and down alternately.

< How to put the monkey on the mountain >

⑩ Insert between triangles.

⑪ Mountain

Monkey

Place the ends a little one upon another as illustrated.

Acrobatic Horse

Chinese traditional origami. Push up the tail with a finger and the horse turns a somersault. It is possible to make it do two somersaults.

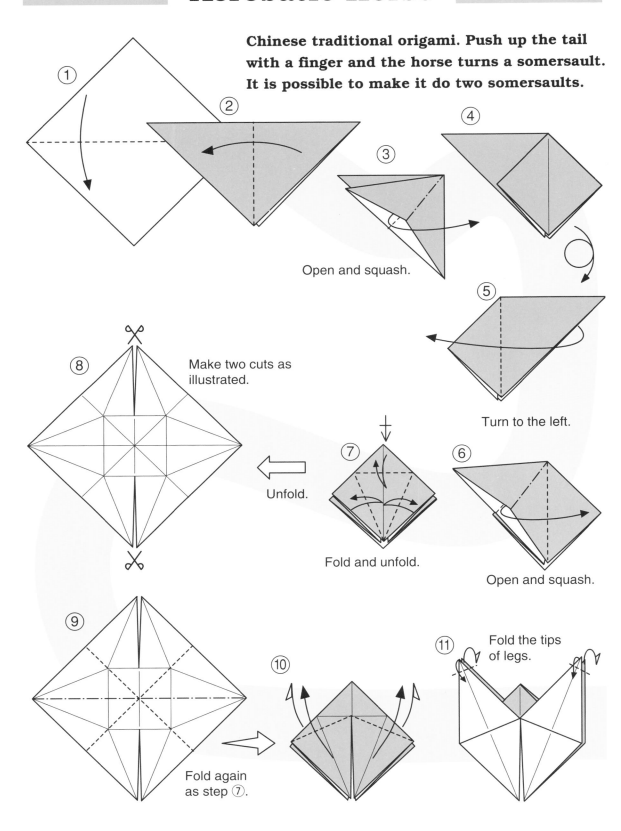

Open and squash.

Turn to the left.

Make two cuts as illustrated.

Unfold.

Fold and unfold.

Open and squash.

Fold again as step ⑦.

Fold the tips of legs.

[For more fun]

Push up the tail with a finger.
The horse turns a somersault
and stands again on the four legs.

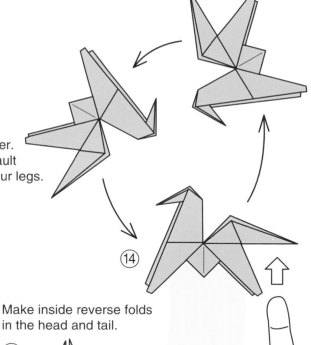

(14)

Make inside reverse folds
in the head and tail.

(13)

a

The tail and line (a)
aligns.

(12)

Mascot Monkey

by Tomoko Fuse

Enjoy by hanging it on a hook.

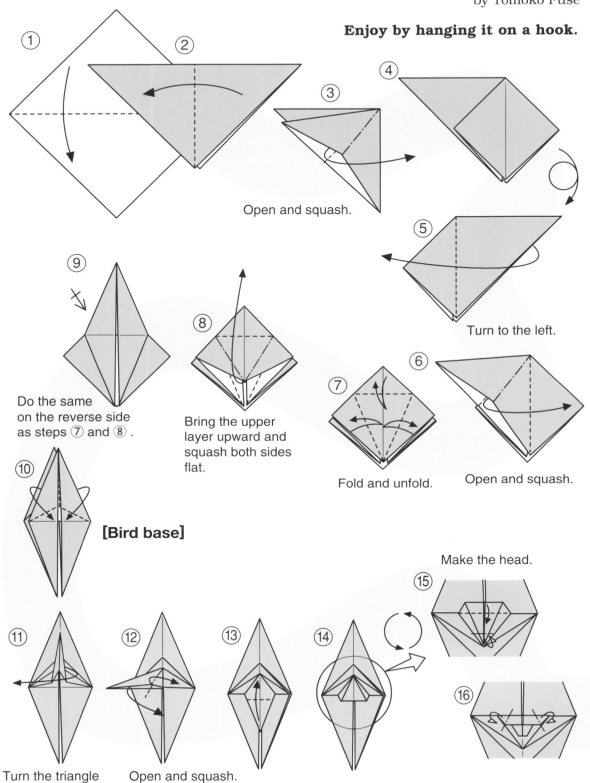

① ②

③ Open and squash.

④

⑤ Turn to the left.

⑥ Open and squash.

⑦ Fold and unfold.

⑧ Bring the upper layer upward and squash both sides flat.

⑨ Do the same on the reverse side as steps ⑦ and ⑧.

⑩ [Bird base]

⑪ Turn the triangle to the left.

⑫ Open and squash.

⑬

⑭

Make the head.

⑮

⑯

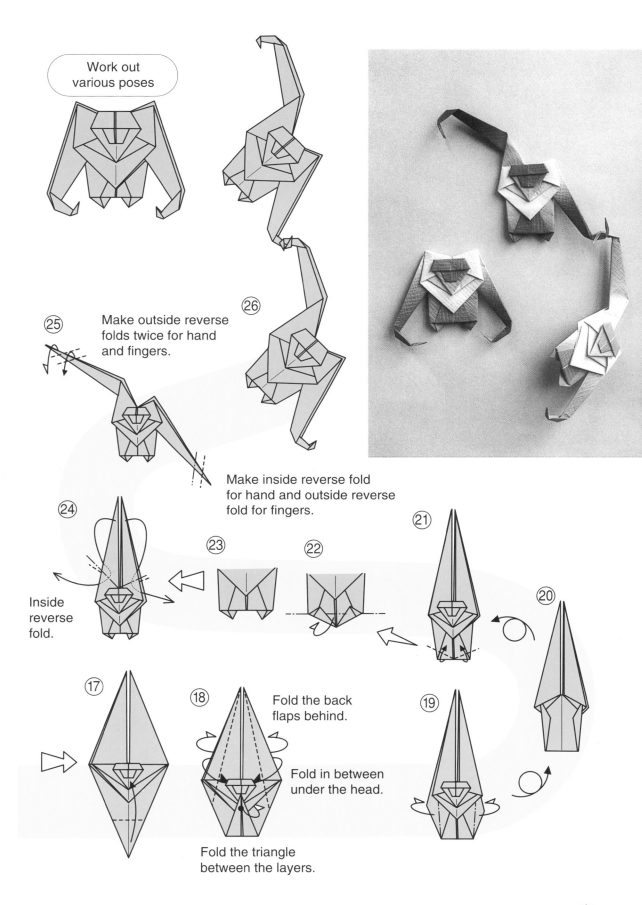

Work out various poses

㉕

㉖

Make outside reverse folds twice for hand and fingers.

Make inside reverse fold for hand and outside reverse fold for fingers.

㉔

Inside reverse fold.

㉓

㉒

㉑

⑳

⑰

⑱

Fold the back flaps behind.

Fold in between under the head.

⑲

Fold the triangle between the layers.

Snail

It is exciting when bulging the shell.

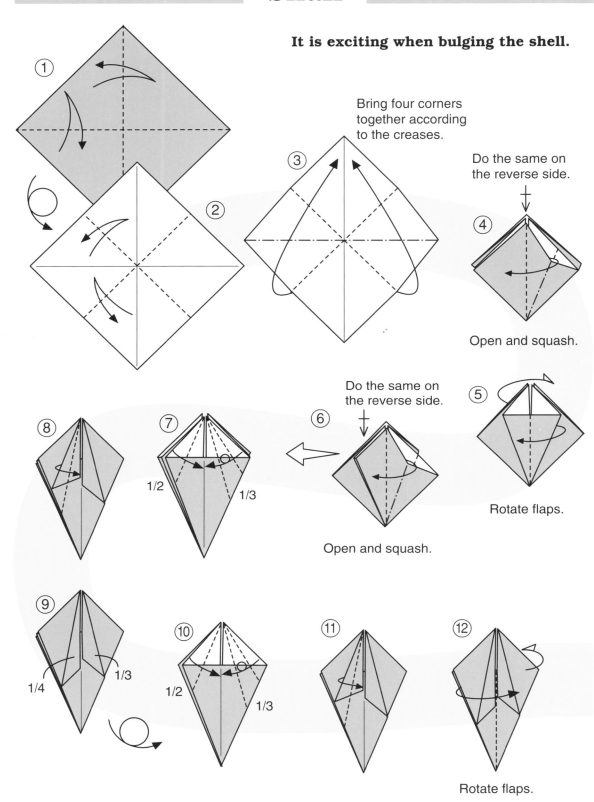

Bring four corners together according to the creases.

Do the same on the reverse side.

Open and squash.

Rotate flaps.

Do the same on the reverse side.

Open and squash.

1/2   1/3

1/4   1/3   1/2   1/3

Rotate flaps.

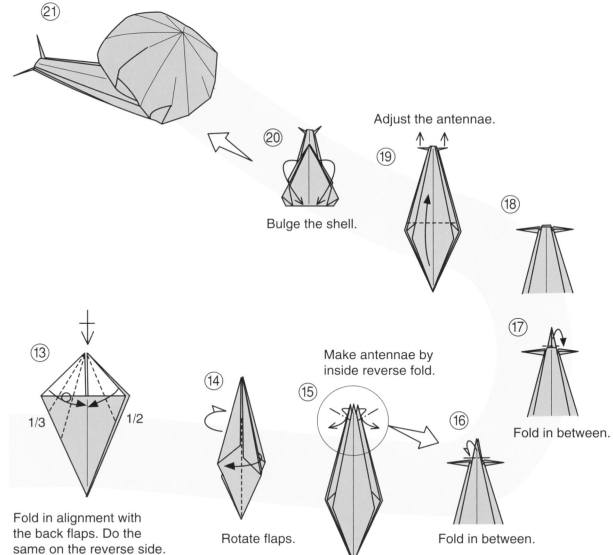

㉑

⑳

Bulge the shell.

Adjust the antennae.

⑲

⑱

⑰

Fold in between.

⑯

Fold in between.

⑮

Make antennae by inside reverse fold.

⑭

Rotate flaps.

⑬

1/3   1/2

Fold in alignment with the back flaps. Do the same on the reverse side.

Water Lily

It is exciting when turning over the petals and letting them stand. Since you have to make many folds, the model tends to become thick. The paper easily tears, so try to use large paper (more than 7 inches square) or a paper napkin or soft paper.

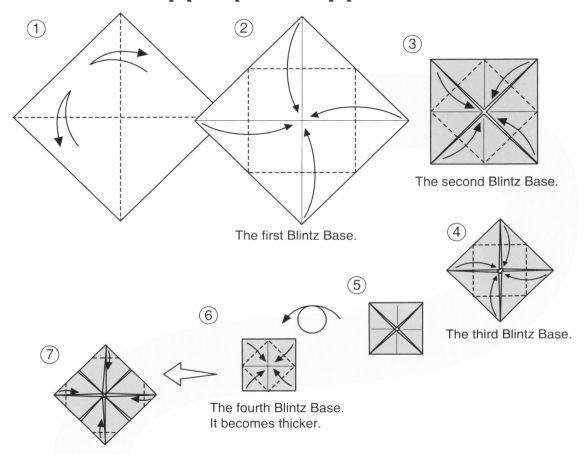

The first Blintz Base.

The second Blintz Base.

The third Blintz Base.

The fourth Blintz Base. It becomes thicker.

Fold the four corners.

Holding the edge, turn over the back flap. Take care not to tear the paper.

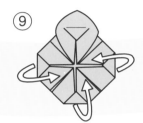

Do the same on the other back flaps.

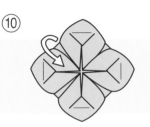

Turn over the back flap.

(16)

(15)

(14)

Turn over each flap
and let it stand.

[View from Top]

(11)

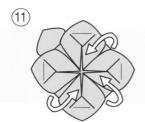

Do the same on the
other back flaps.

(12)

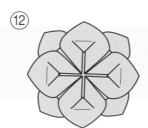

[View from Side]

(13)

This is completed, but
if you try to turn over
the remaining back flaps,
it becomes gorgeous.

Iris & Lily

The same body changes to an iris or a lily, depending on the folding of petals.

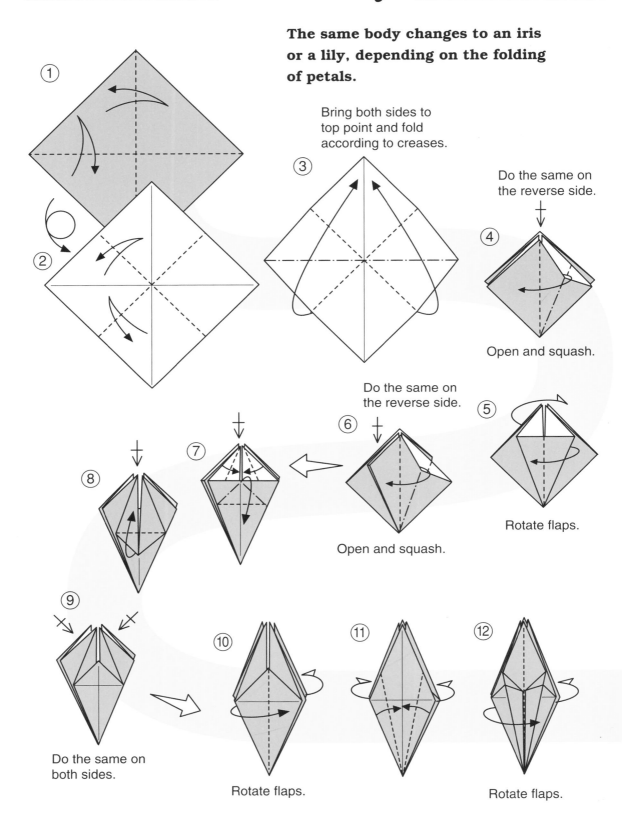

Bring both sides to top point and fold according to creases.

Do the same on the reverse side.

Open and squash.

Do the same on the reverse side.

Rotate flaps.

Open and squash.

Do the same on both sides.

Rotate flaps.

Rotate flaps.

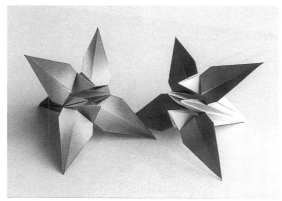

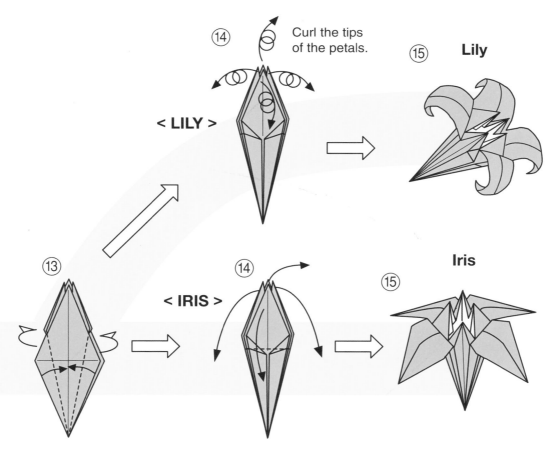

⑭ Curl the tips
of the petals.

< LILY >

⑮ **Lily**

⑬

< IRIS >

⑭

⑮ **Iris**

Balloon

Blow up the completed balloon.

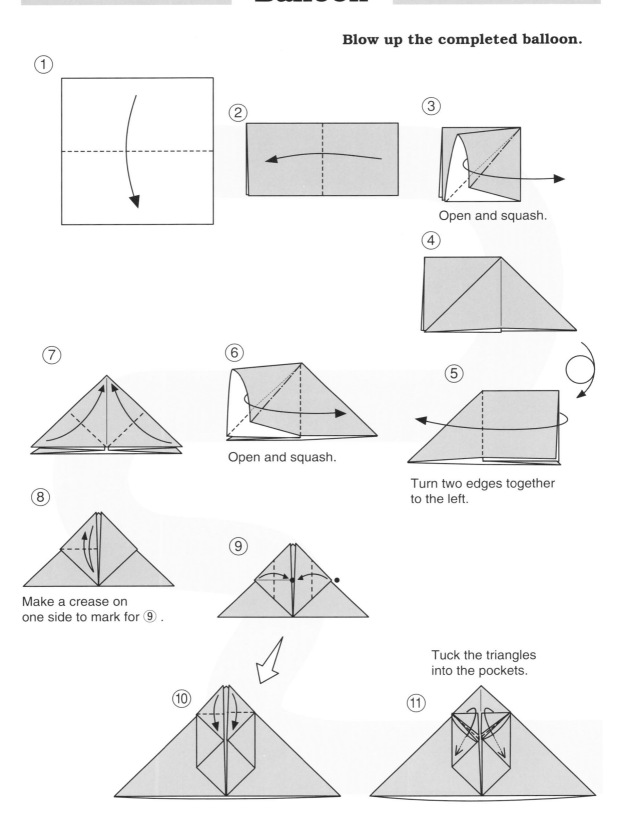

①

②

③ Open and squash.

④

⑤ Turn two edges together to the left.

⑥ Open and squash.

⑦

⑧ Make a crease on one side to mark for ⑨.

⑨

⑩

⑪ Tuck the triangles into the pockets.

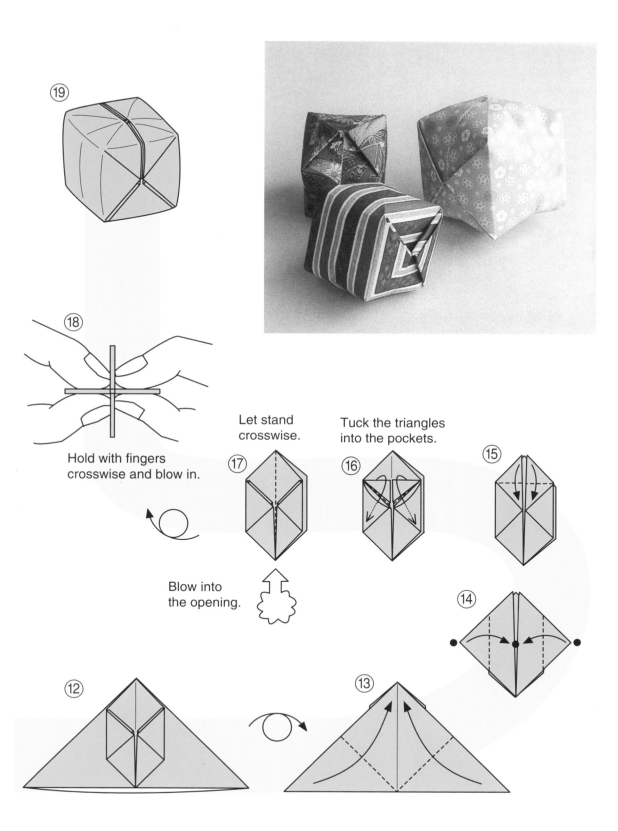

⑲

⑱

Hold with fingers
crosswise and blow in.

Let stand
crosswise.

⑰

Tuck the triangles
into the pockets.

⑯

⑮

Blow into
the opening.

⑭

⑫

⑬

Wild Hare

Fold one side of the balloon in the shape of ears.

Begin with step ⑬ of
the balloon (on page 59).
(Start with color side up.)

①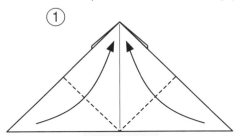

②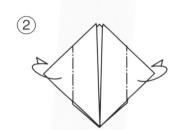

Fold back
in between.

③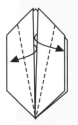

⑦

⑥

Blow into
the opening.

④

⑤

60

Santa Claus

by Tomoko Fuse

**Very simple and easy Santa Claus.
You can change the size of the face in step ④.**

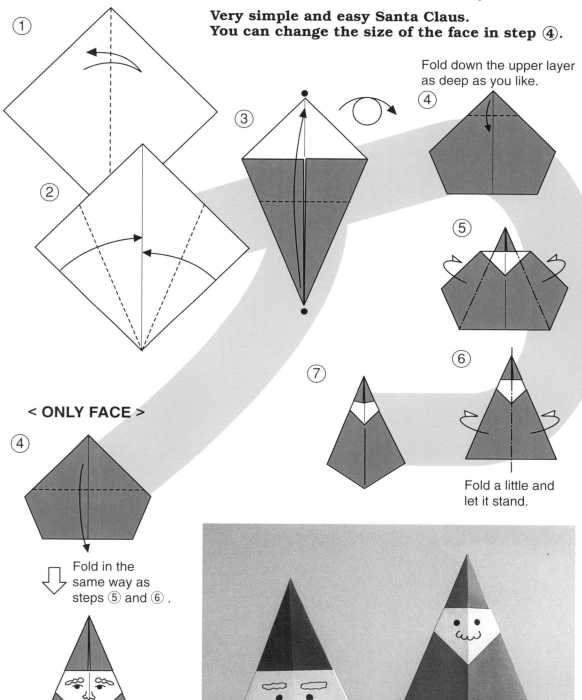

① ②

③

④ Fold down the upper layer as deep as you like.

⑤

⑥ Fold a little and let it stand.

⑦

< ONLY FACE >

④

Fold in the same way as steps ⑤ and ⑥.

It is fun to draw the face.

Hat of Santa Claus

by Tomoko Fuse

This hat is suitable for a christmas tree ornament.

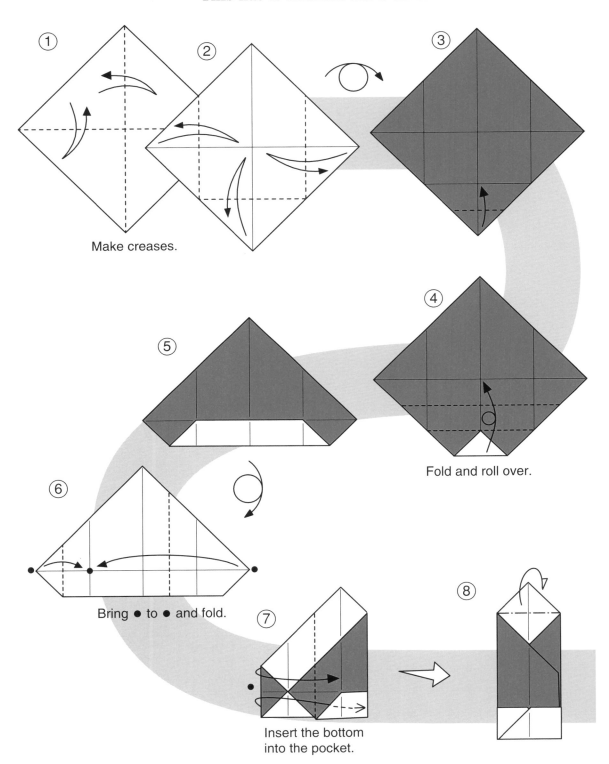

Make creases.

Fold and roll over.

Bring ● to ● and fold.

Insert the bottom
into the pocket.

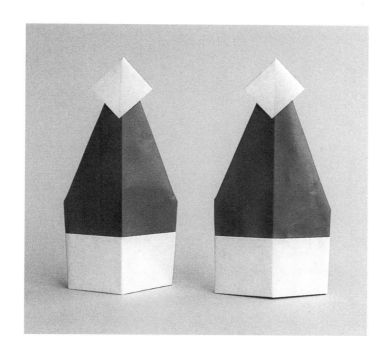

⑬

⑫

Lightly
press.

Insert a finger into the opening
and shape it like a cylinder.

⑨

Fold inside layers only.

⑩

⑪

(Process of folding)

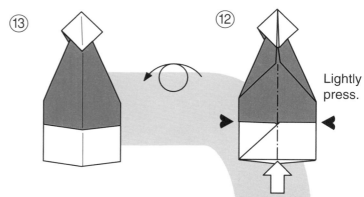

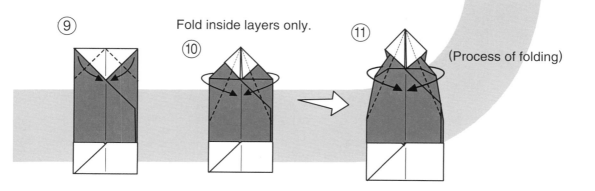

Shoes of Santa Claus

by Tomoko Fuse

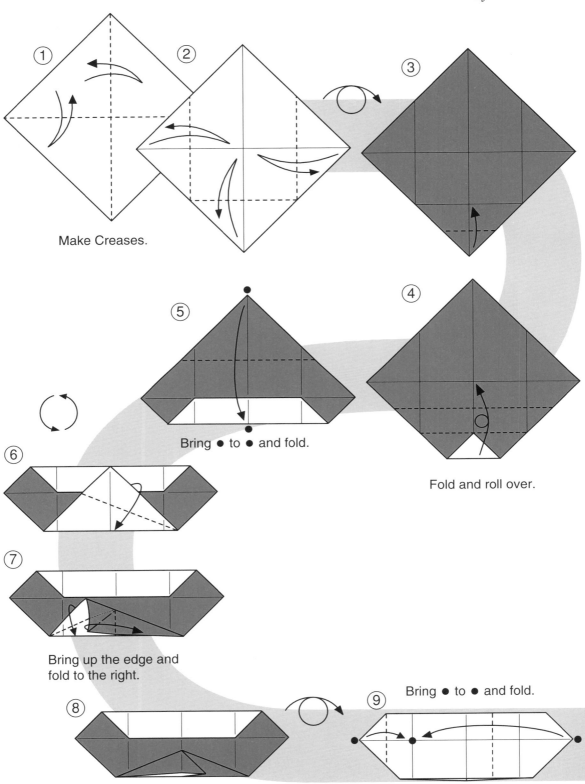

Make Creases.

Bring ● to ● and fold.

Fold and roll over.

Bring up the edge and fold to the right.

Bring ● to ● and fold.

You can make an outside reverse fold at the tip.

Outside reverse fold.

Fold in half and insert the edge into the pockets.

⑩

⑪ Press lightly.

Insert a finger into the opening and shape it like a cylinder.

⑫ Inside reverse fold.

⑬

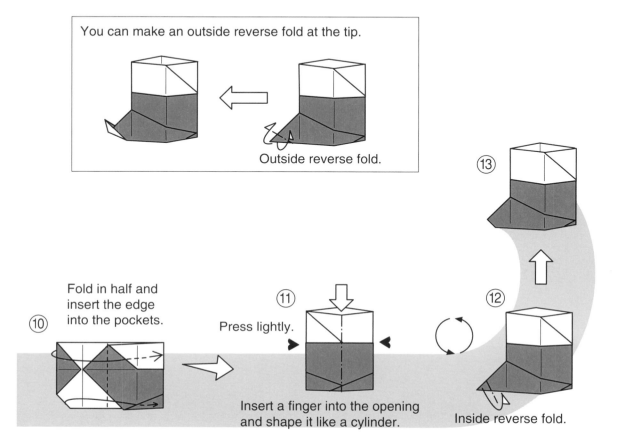

Crown

by Tomoko Fuse

**If you use shiny paper,
you can make a fantastic crown.**

Make creases
on color side.

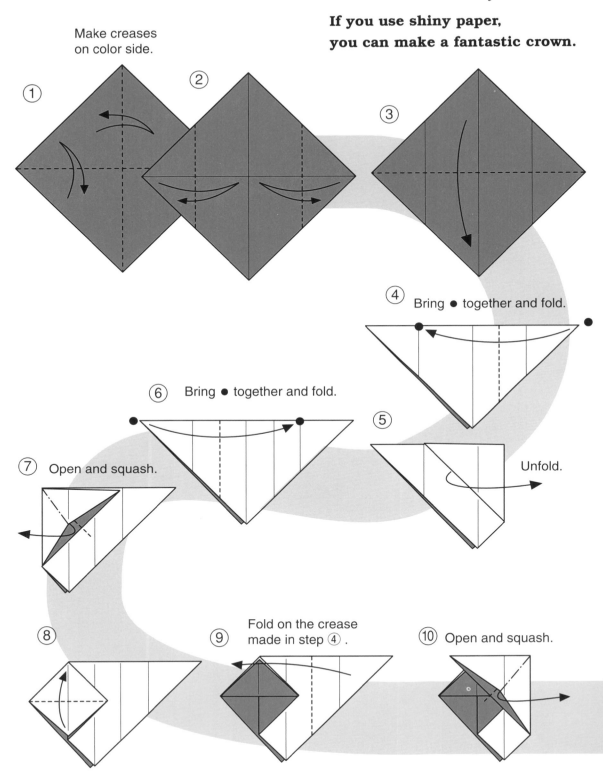

① ②

③

④ Bring ● together and fold.

⑥ Bring ● together and fold.

⑤

Unfold.

⑦ Open and squash.

⑧

⑨ Fold on the crease
made in step ④.

⑩ Open and squash.

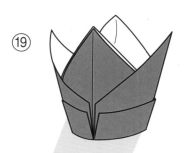

⑲

Open the bottom and
dent the top.

⑱

⑰

⑯

Bring ● together and fold.

⑮ Fold in numerical order.

1   2

⑭

⑪

⑫ Bring ● together
and fold.

⑬

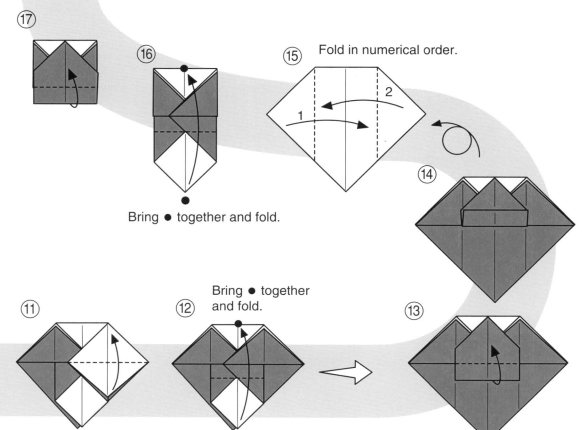

Hunting Cap

by Tomoko Fuse

A cap that suits Sherlock Holmes.

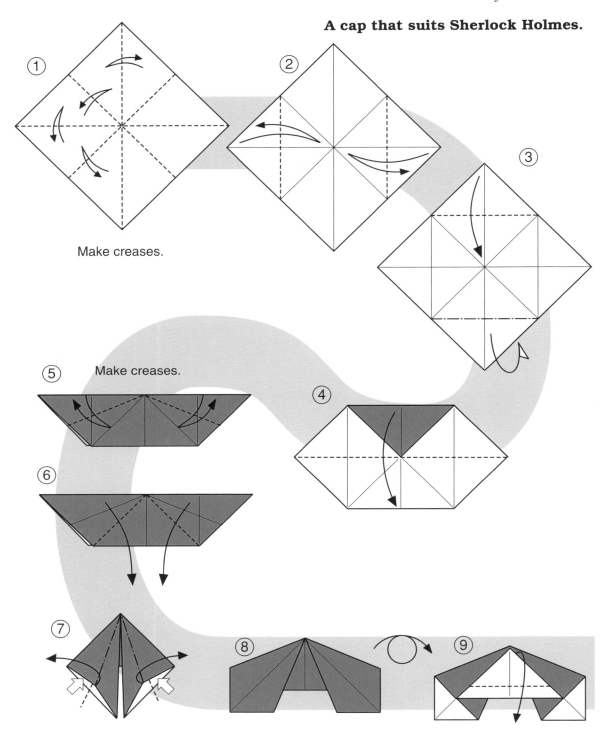

① Make creases.

②

③

④

⑤ Make creases.

⑥

⑦ Open and squash along the creases made in step ⑤.

⑧

⑨ Fold down to make the visor.

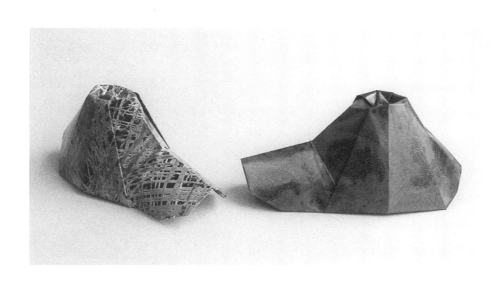

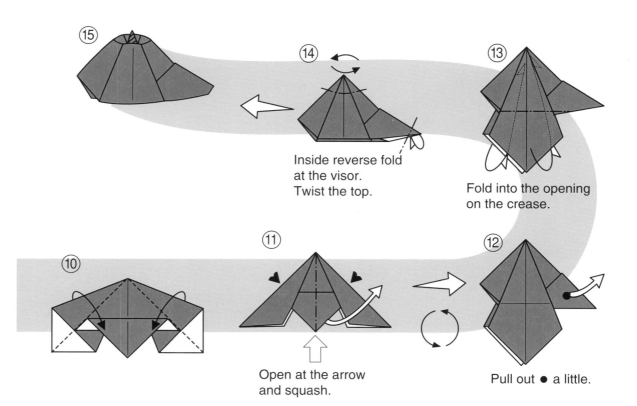

⑮

⑭
Inside reverse fold
at the visor.
Twist the top.

⑬
Fold into the opening
on the crease.

⑩

⑪
Open at the arrow
and squash.

⑫
Pull out ● a little.

Tomoko's Cat

by Tomoko Fuse

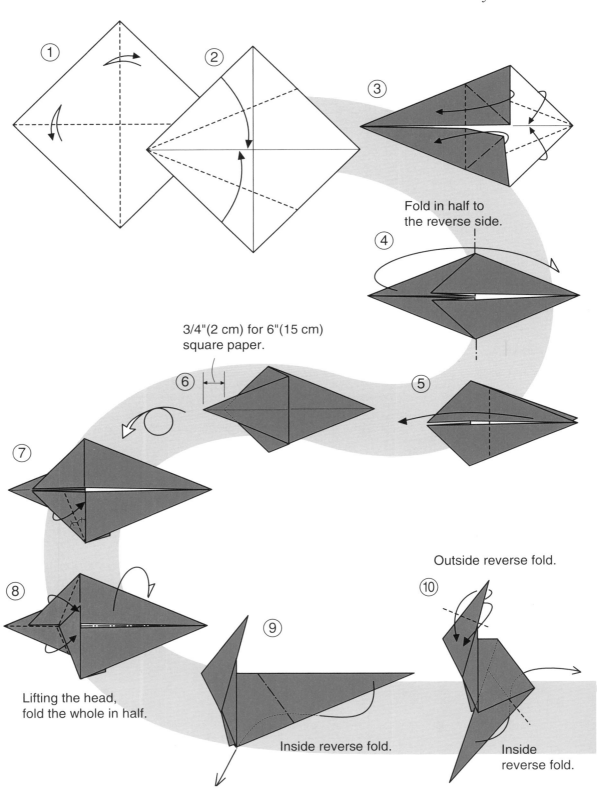

Fold in half to the reverse side.

3/4"(2 cm) for 6"(15 cm) square paper.

Lifting the head, fold the whole in half.

Inside reverse fold.

Outside reverse fold.

Inside reverse fold.

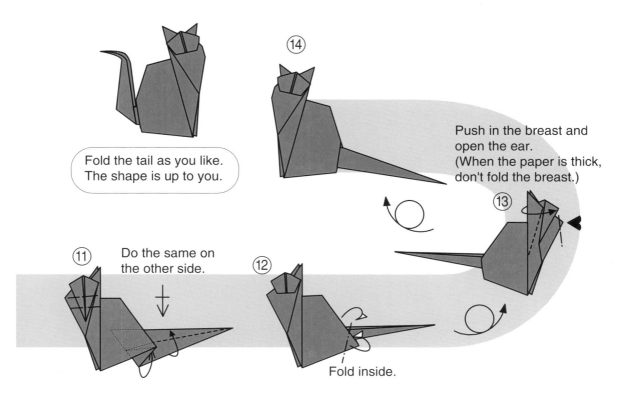

Fold the tail as you like.
The shape is up to you.

⑭

Push in the breast and
open the ear.
(When the paper is thick,
don't fold the breast.)

⑬

⑪ Do the same on
the other side.

⑫

Fold inside.

Double Stars

by Tomoko Fuse

Join two stars. The stars are the same on both sides.

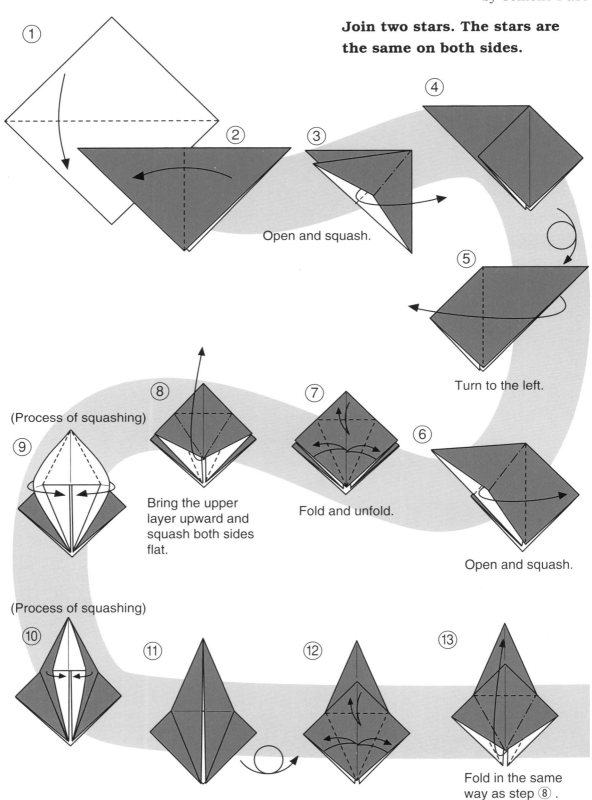

①

②

③ Open and squash.

④

⑤ Turn to the left.

⑥ Open and squash.

⑦ Fold and unfold.

⑧ Bring the upper layer upward and squash both sides flat.

⑨ (Process of squashing)

⑩ (Process of squashing)

⑪

⑫

⑬ Fold in the same way as step ⑧.

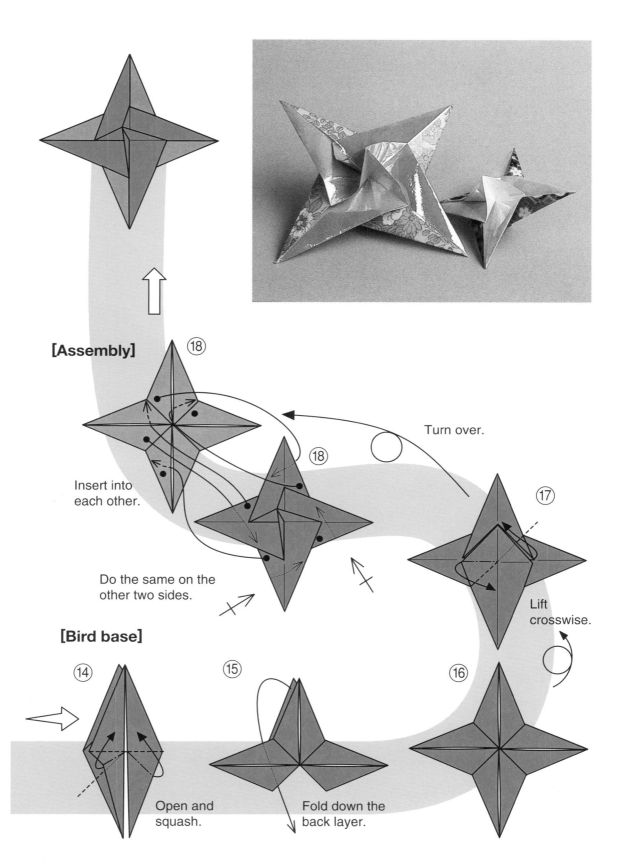

[Assembly]

⑱

⑱

Turn over.

Insert into
each other.

⑰

Do the same on the
other two sides.

Lift
crosswise.

[Bird base]

⑭

⑮

⑯

Open and
squash.

Fold down the
back layer.

Strawberry

by Tomoko Fuse

**Blow up the completed strawberry.
It looks like a ripe strawberry.**

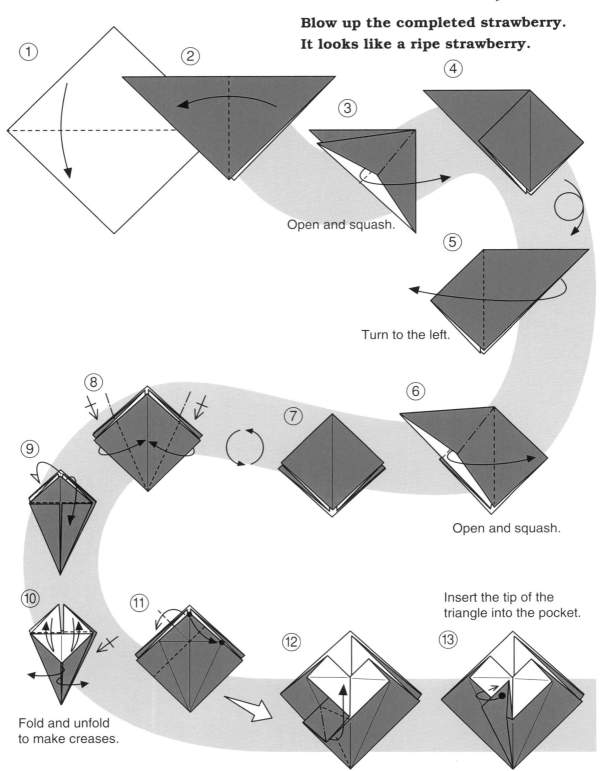

① ②

③

Open and squash.

④

⑤

Turn to the left.

⑥

Open and squash.

⑦

⑧

⑨

⑩

Fold and unfold
to make creases.

⑪

⑫

⑬

Insert the tip of the
triangle into the pocket.

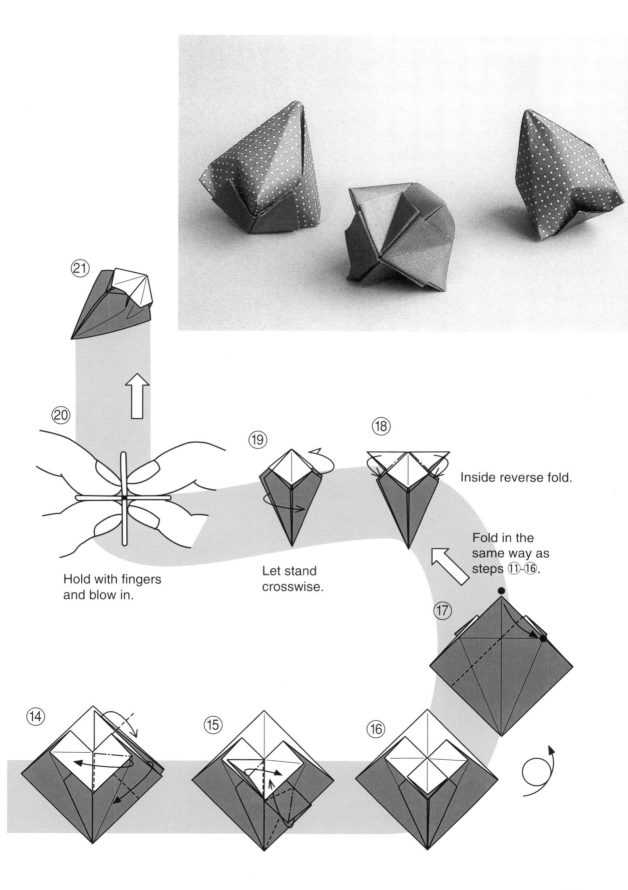

㉑

⑳

Hold with fingers
and blow in.

⑲

Let stand
crosswise.

⑱

Inside reverse fold.

Fold in the
same way as
steps ⑪-⑯.

⑰

⑭

⑮

⑯

Helmet & Goldfish

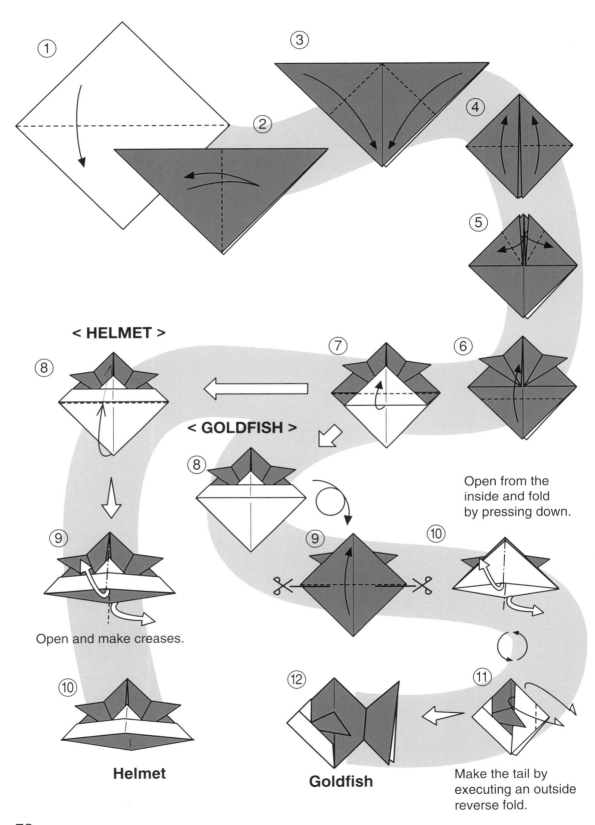

① ② ③ ④ ⑤ ⑥ ⑦

< HELMET >

⑧ ⑨ ⑩

< GOLDFISH >

⑧ ⑨ ⑩ ⑪ ⑫

Open and make creases.

Open from the inside and fold by pressing down.

Helmet

Goldfish

Make the tail by executing an outside reverse fold.

Lovely Pig

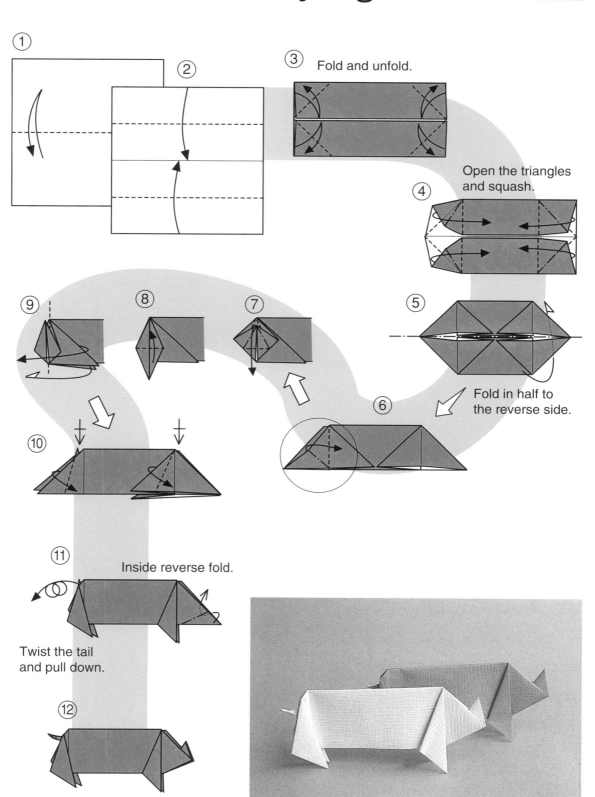

①

②

③ Fold and unfold.

④ Open the triangles and squash.

⑤ Fold in half to the reverse side.

⑥

⑦

⑧

⑨

⑩

⑪ Inside reverse fold.

Twist the tail and pull down.

⑫

Chopstick Bag

by Tomoko Fuse

The standard size of paper
is 8 1/2" x 11"(letter-size).

A chopstick bag with a fan.
The width of pleats is not fixed.
Use paper as long as you like.

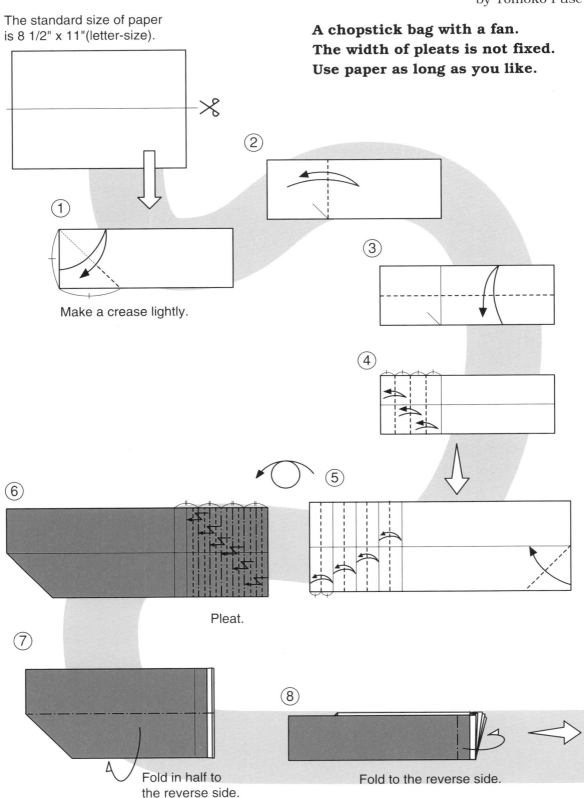

① Make a crease lightly.

②

③

④

⑤

⑥ Pleat.

⑦ Fold in half to
the reverse side.

⑧ Fold to the reverse side.

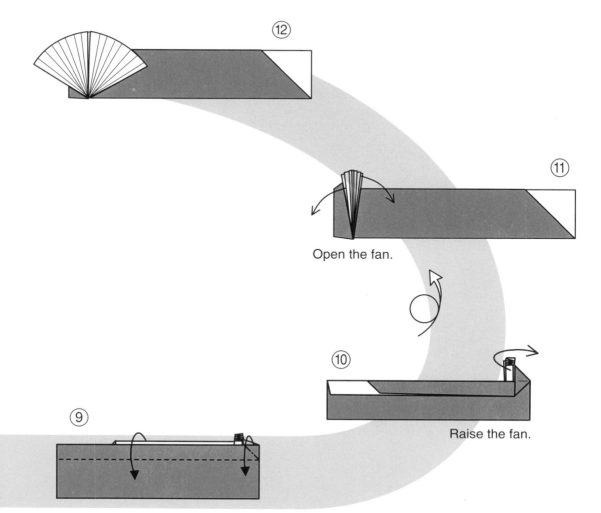

⑫

⑪

Open the fan.

⑩

Raise the fan.

⑨

Fox Mask

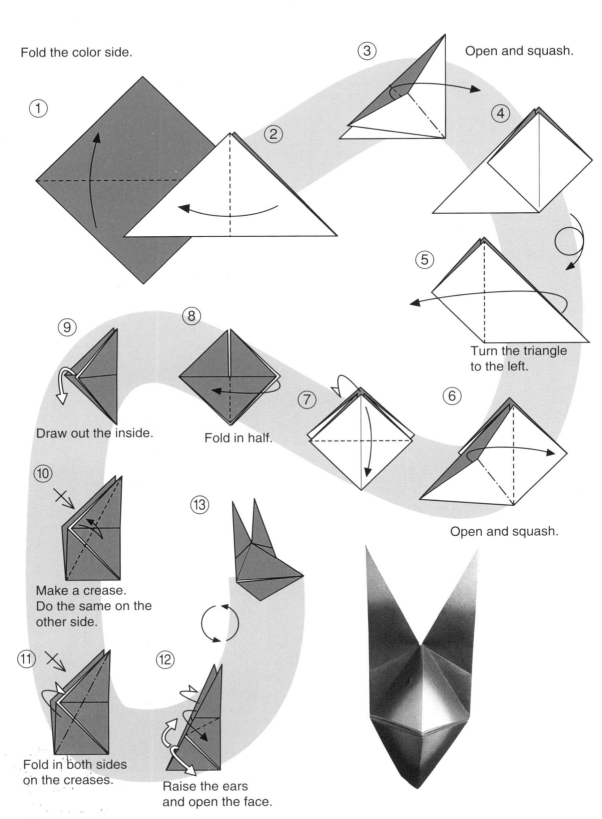

Fold the color side.

①

②

③ Open and squash.

④

⑤ Turn the triangle to the left.

⑥ Open and squash.

⑦

⑧ Fold in half.

⑨ Draw out the inside.

⑩ Make a crease. Do the same on the other side.

⑪ Fold in both sides on the creases.

⑫ Raise the ears and open the face.

⑬